YOGA FOR BACKACHE

Elaine Mackay

By the same authors

YOGA FOR WOMEN

ESSENCE OF YOGA

YOGA OVER FORTY

Contents

Introduction

In selecting yoga exercises and *asanas* to help overcome backache, our difficulty has not been to find enough to include but to decide what to exclude. In a book of this size there must be a limit; yet in yoga training almost everything relates back to the spine or spinal nerves, for this area is regarded as a vital source of good health and continued youth.

There is also the fact that many backaches do not originate in the spine itself but come from pressure or distortion in other parts of the body. Though yoga has remedies for many of these conditions it is impossible to describe them all. We have included the most essential ... relaxation of nervous tension, improvement of elimination, abdominal breathing and a few of the most important *asanas* (bodily positions) that influence the general health.

This leads to the obvious conclusions that the practice of yoga helps to maintain spinal health and freedom from backache; and that no backache should be regarded as a purely local condition. The source must be sought and found before any treatment is given. Many causes are never really defined, suggesting psychosomatic origins, in which cases yoga has always proved a great help; and even when the cause is physical, if there is nothing to forbid it, the exercises and *asanas* given in this book will strengthen and benefit the spine, and consequently the health of the whole body.

THE AUTHORS

Sydney

I

The Spine and Yoga

Hundreds of lives are affected, millions of man-hours lost every year all over the world through backache. Many books and articles have been written on the subject and it is constantly discussed; yet because it is so common and because normally it is not a killer there is still a tendency to regard it as a disability to be endured rather than an ailment that should be cured. People put up with it through apathy, exhaustion or ignorance, or accept it as an inevitable symptom of ageing.

This is a defeatist attitude. Though it is true that a cure has not yet been found for some back conditions, many could be rectified if the sufferer exerted himself to seek help, whether from physicians, surgeons, osteopaths, naturopaths or even from himself or herself. One of the best forms of self-help is found in yoga training.

In the authors' experience there have been many cases in which benefits have been derived from yoga after orthodox medical treatment failed to give relief.

In *hatha* yoga, which might be described as the philosophy of physical well-being, a healthy spine is considered essential and much time is devoted to achieving and maintaining spinal health. Many exercises and *asanas* (bodily poses) are expressly designed to strengthen and improve the backbone. The ancient sages knew that it was not merely a prop for supporting the head but a complex instrument that must be cared for; that its neglect or abuse could affect the health of the whole body; that its deterioration was the beginning of old age. They knew that it contained and protected the spinal cord, upon which our lives depend, and which, to the advanced yogi, is a medium for developing his higher faculties.

Structure of the spine

The spine, known as *Meru Danda* in Sanscrit, is a column of 33 bones or vertebrae, running from the base of the skull to the lowest part of the back. The vertebrae are usually referred to in five sections: cervical or neck (7 bones); dorsal-thoracic (12 bones); lumbar or waist (5 bones); sacral or hips (5 bones) and coccygeal or tail vertebrae (4 bones).

Between each vertebra is a pad or disc. These discs, which are soft and resilient, help to cushion the spine – and indirectly the brain and whole nervous system – from sudden shocks and jars. They also prevent the bones from grating against each other in movement and, with appropriate muscles and ligaments, facilitate bodily flexibility.

The vertebrae are hollow and their position one upon the other forms a canal through which runs the *spinal cord*. This, with the brain, forms the *Central Nervous System*. From between the vertebrae small bundles of nerves go out from the spinal cord to different parts of the body.

On each side of the spine are a chain of nerve fibres. This is the *Sympathetic Nervous System*, which controls the inner life of the body ... respiration, digestion, circulation, etc. In normal health these nerves carry on their work without conscious direction from the brain.

Though both Central and Sympathetic Nervous Systems are autonomous they are interdependent. Loss of vitality or health in one affects the other.

It is by developing complete control over the Sympathetic Nervous System that yogis in advanced stages of development can perform extraordinary feats: stopping the heart; surviving burial for long periods; acceleration of healing processes.

The spine is thus one of the most important parts of the body, yet it is often the most neglected. We know that death or paralysis may result if it is severely damaged by illness or accident; but many painful and crippling conditions may arise from ordinary neglect and carelessness. Not only is the health of the spine affected by the body; the body is also affected by the health of the spine.

Yoga is not a miracle cure-all and no fantastic claims are made for its remedial powers; but because of its emphasis on the care and health of the spine it improves and in many cases cures back troubles.

Before any attempt is made at treating backache through *hatha* yoga – or any other means – a full understanding of the complaint is imperative. The pain may stem from a disorder that requires absolute rest, such as kidney or liver complaints, or from the acute condition of a slipped disc, in which case exercise is the very worst thing. It is always advisable to get a medical opinion. Many doctors now are acquainted with yoga and can say whether or not it may be safely practised.

There are certain cautions and prohibitions to be observed in different cases. The fact that they are repeated throughout this book should emphasise their importance.

Students who have had a slipped disc must be careful not to force or strain the spine, specially in forward-stretching movements. Abrupt jerks must be avoided.

Those over fifty who are quite unused to physical activity; those who are in bad physical condition; those who are much overweight, even if young, should be very careful, not undertaking strenuous exercises and not standing on the head until health and weight are improved.

Women suffering from prolapse of the uterus should not practice strenuous raised poses ... the crab, peacock, bird, etc.

Asanas should never be practised 'cold' ... The muscles must be warmed up gradually with preliminary exercises and gentle manipulation.

In all cases of vague unidentified back pains, try to establish the basic cause before attempting to cure them through yoga.

2

Causes of Backache

Backaches could be divided, generally, into those originating in the spine or back, and those caused by disturbance in other parts of the body but manifesting in the back. The latter are far in excess of the former and frequently come from the way we live.

It is remarkable how much the ancient sages knew of anatomy. They also identified many of the causes of backache long before our modern osteopaths discovered them.

Common ailments of the spine and back
Slipped disc

This term is now so fashionable that it would seem half the population have slipped discs. It is used to describe almost any kind of back pain.

In genuine cases of slipped disc, one of the cushioning discs or pads between the vertebrae is torn or pushed out of position, putting pressure on nerves and causing extreme pain and complete loss of movement in the area. A fall, jerk or sudden strain, even a simple movement at a moment when the spine is not prepared could displace a disc; and it often occurs when the general spinal health is poor. Unsuitable diet, inadequate rest, lack of exercise or occupations involving constant unnatural posture all

13

weaken the spine. (For instance, a round-shouldered sedentary worker whose spine has become bent forward could displace a disc through sudden jerking or lifting).

While in the acute stage, exercise is out of the question, but a knowledge of relaxation and practice of *advasana* (page 45), helps to release the painful muscular spasm that follows displacement of the disc.

Many doctors recommend yogic exercises after the acute condition has subsided, for strengthening the spine and muscles of the back and preventing repetition of the trouble. The patient must practice carefully, avoiding any kind of jerking, specially in forward-stretching movements.

Rheumatism

Rheumatism shows itself in different forms but is generally recognised by stiffness and – usually – pain in the muscles and fibrous cartilages. It occurs in any part of the body, from head to feet. Medical opinion is still undecided on its source though relative acidity of the body is believed to contribute.

The word rheumatism is mainly used for the condition in general. When it is in the lower back or lumbar region it is often called Lumbago. Lumbago may be brought on by chills, over-fatigue or muscular strain.

When people speak of Rheumatoid Arthritis they are usually referring to a condition in the bony joints. There is inflammation and swelling in the joints and later complete loss of movement through destruction of the cartilage between the bones; even actual fusion of the bones themselves.

Sometimes the muscles or cartilages round or covering

the joint are affected but not the joint itself. In these cases, which are often diagnosed as rheumatoid arthritis, mobility is not lost and the sufferer could help himself by rest, improved elimination, massage, diet and suitable exercise.

We repeat that yoga makes no claim to *cure* arthritis; but it can and does help to slow down the progress of the disease by raising the general health and keeping the body mobile. It is generally accepted that we are more susceptible to infectious diseases when we are run down, but we often overlook the fact that the same applies to non-infectious diseases.

An important weapon in fighting this condition is the will to help oneself and a determination to persevere, though movement is painful and laborious. The alternative could be eventual complete immobility.

Sciatica is inflammation of the sciatic nerve. It is painful and persistent and is best treated by rest, correction of diet, massage and appropriate exercise. Certain yoga *asanas* are recommended for sciatica, having direct and beneficial effect on the sciatic nerve. These poses are: *Spinal Twist; Little Twist; Archer, and Forward-Stretching cycle.*

Pain in the pelvic joints

This form of backache is usually caused by a displacement of the sacro-iliac joints, which are put under strain. The slightest deviation from their correct position may be reflected in other parts of the body – as for example in bad headaches. Any suspicion of this trouble should be properly investigated before an attempt is made to correct it through exercise.

Curvature

Extreme inward curve in the small of the back comes from an inherent spinal weakness. The whole posture is affected, organs are displaced and pressure put on nerves and blood vessels. Yoga training will strengthen the back muscles and often helps to improve the condition.

Growing pains

The use of this term, now fortunately almost obsolete, is a dangerous and shortsighted way of dismissing backache in children. Since there are no such things as growing pains, all pains in the back should be traced to their source, and if there is nothing to forbid it, the young and growing spine strengthened and developed by correct exercise.

Other causes of backache

When the backache arises from disorder in another part of the body, the original cause must be removed before the back itself can benefit, however faithfully you exercise and strengthen it through yoga. An inflamed kidney affecting the small of the back or flat feet throwing the body out of balance will negate all your efforts; but when elimination of the basic cause is accompanied by yoga training there could be quite spectacular improvement in health and well-being as well as freedom from crippling pain.

Yoga spinal training is advised for the types of backache listed below – unless forbidden by a doctor or the nature of the illness itself. In many cases yoga will also improve the basic cause.

Nervous tension

Overwork, frustration, the constant driving of tired nerves and body, leading to inability to relax, could all show up in an aching back. It is a vicious cycle. The backache leads to irritability, insomnia and further nervous strain, which increase the pain and tension. Many sufferers never connect cause and effect and waste time on useless remedies for the back while ignoring the root of the trouble; others become addicted to sedatives and sleeping pills which dull the pain but do not cure it and result in a general deterioration of the nervous system.

Stress and worry

We are told that stress, worry, anxiety can cause muscle spasm. This is a contraction or shortening of the muscles which puts strain and pressure on nerves and blood-vessels and is felt either as a violent cramp, or more often as less acute aches and pains.

When, as so often happens, the conditions causing the trouble are beyond the sufferer's control, his only recourse is to do what he can to help his body withstand them. This includes attention to diet, exercise and rest, and – vitally important – developing the ability to completely relax muscles, nerves and mind at will; to wipe out all troubling thoughts and through yoga breathing to recharge the system with vitality.

Psychosomatic causes

Deep mental and emotional disturbances often express themselves indirectly through physical ailments. Guilt, fear, grief, etc., could all result in a chronically aching back; a generally dissatisfied attitude to life could take the form of constant nagging pain. Though improvement of the general health through relaxation, rest and exercise is an important help in these cases the trouble will not be completely cured until the state of mind causing it is corrected.

It may be necessary to achieve a different attitude to life, to change the whole scale of values; or, when the trouble lies deep in the sufferer's own personality, to overcome the weakness or destructive tendencies by developing inner strength. This is not easy. It is a long and difficult process; but it could lead not only to freedom from physical affliction but to inner freedom . . . a new mental and emotional health that may change a life. It is available to all who have the courage to work for it.

Reflected pains

It is foolish to think that every pain in the lower back comes from Bright's Disease or cirrhosis of the liver; but it is also foolish to ignore the possibilities that severe, sickening and dragging pains in this area could be reflected from internal organs. Establish the source by medical examination before attempting self-help through exercise, for rest is essential in such cases. There is also the possibility of heightened blood pressure which would prohibit the practice of certain *asanas*.

Should the backache be caused by organic disease, yoga practice should be confined to relaxation, breathing cycles and mental exercises. *Colitis* and *Ulcers*, which are often an outcome of nervous or emotional stress, could give rise to backache. As in the case of liver and kidney disorders, relaxation, deep breathing and mental exercises to develop serenity will all bring positive help.

Posture

It has been suggested that man stood upright too soon in his evolution; that the effort of balancing on two feet instead of standing squarely on four strains bones, organs and nerves. However that may be, the spine in two-footed creatures has had to assume the additional function of keeping the body upright. In this it fights a constant battle against the forces of central gravity which, while holding us to the earth's surface, also exert a downward pull on the whole organism. The effects of gravity, so well known to the ancient yogis, is often overlooked in the treatment of modern maladies.

This is one reason why standing for long periods is so tiring. When the posture is bad the strain on the spine is increased; the nerve fibres and muscles attached to it are affected. If the neck and back are held in one straight line – as taught in yoga – the head is carried comfortably by the spinal column, but when it is poked forward muscles and spine must strain to support the weight. The vertebrae could become displaced and nerves and blood vessels subjected to pressure. Similarly, if the stomach is constantly protruded the back takes the strain, as in pregnancy, since it is the back wall of the abdominal cavity.

Weak, neglected, underdeveloped back muscles, sloppiness in sitting and standing will cause and increase bad posture. Fortunately it is a habit that responds to yoga training, specially to spinal exercises and to stretching and balancing *asanas*.

A more serious contributing cause of bad posture is arthritis or rheumatism in other parts of the body. Pain or stiffness in feet, legs, hips may cause change of posture and loss of balance, resulting in strain on the spine and back muscles.

Flat feet. High heels. Foot ailments

Since the feet are the base of the body and govern the balance, the spine is affected by any abnormality they may develop.

Flat feet contribute to wrong posture; so do high heels, which throw the body forward unnaturally; tight shoes, corns and bunions which inhibit normal walking. In trying to avoid pressure on the painful spot the sufferer upsets his balance, so that muscles and ligaments must strain to restore it.

If the basic cause of the strain is corrected, yoga *asanas*, including the balancing poses, and the foot and leg exercises, will restore the balance and repair the general damage.

Haemorrhoids (Piles)

Pain in the lower back could come from haemorrhoids. This condition may be ameliorated by practice of *aswini-mudra* – contraction of the rectal muscles (page 62), the inverted poses (page 63), the cycle of abdominal contractions for overcoming constipation (pages 64, 65) and by correction of diet.

Enlargement of the prostate gland

This occurs usually in older men and also contributes to backache. In the early stages the shoulderstand (page

63) and *aswini-mudra* are recommended. If the trouble persists medical treatment should be sought.

Menstrual Backache

These dragging and exhausting pains in the back regularly endured by many women are greatly relieved by a knowledge of relaxation and the toning-up of the glands, especially the sex glands. The pains often disappear after the health has been improved through general yoga practice but special attention should be given to the shoulderstand, and *asanas* benefiting the female reproductive system. These include the Bow, Cobra, Spinal Twist, *Aswini-mudra*, Lotus Position and the abdominal contractions, *Uddiyana* and *Nauli*.

Pregnancy and post-natal backaches

Regular and correct prenatal exercising will strengthen the back muscles under strain during pregnancy and help them support the extra weight they must carry. When the back is strong there is rarely post-natal backache. With the doctor's approval, pregnant women could practice Pose of a Cat (page 51), Lotus position (page 62), modified Pose of a Fish (page 49) and relaxing movements for the hips (page 36).

For post-natal backache include also the exercises for strengthening the back and those for the abdominal muscles in Chapter Four.

Prolapse of the uterus

Caused by muscular weakness and strain in child-bearing, this is often reflected in dragging back pains. The condition will be improved by the shoulderstand, *aswini-*

mudra, and exercises for strengthening the stomach muscles.

Women yoga students with prolapse should not practice raised poses.

Overeating

This causes backache through pressure of the distended stomach on nerves or by affecting the posture and straining the back muscles. *Constipation* has the same effect when the overloaded bowels press upon nerves and tissues in the back. All these complaints will benefit from relaxation, exercise, diet, fasting and the cycle of stomach contractions.

Occupational fatigue

Standing. Chronic backache is common among dentists, shop assistants, traffic police, housewives who spend all day on their feet. After posture, shoes, diet and beds have been checked, and corrected if necessary, *savasana* (pages 26–27) and all the inverted poses should be practised as often as possible.

Sitting. Typists, sedentary workers in general should try to strengthen the spine so that they may dispense with supports and work for long periods if necessary without tired or aching backs. The arms and shoulders should be exercised, all limbering-up and stretching movements practised. Backaches in such occupations could spring from boredom and dissatisfaction with monotonous work.

Driving. Taxi, bus and truck drivers frequently complain of backache. This is not only due to muscular weakness but to the nervous tension involved. Such sufferers would be relieved by learning to relax, learning deep breathing, and while driving, supporting the aching back with a cushion until exercise has strengthened it.

3

The Spine in Yoga Training

Much of a yogi's physical training is concentrated on the spine.

A yoga proverb says that *Old Age comes with Stiffening of the Backbone,* and we all know that one of the commonest signs of ageing is loss of flexibility in back and joints; but there is a deeper meaning behind the saying. Yoga teaches that old age is a combination of bodily changes which not only cause stiffness but also affect the roots of the spinal nerves, the Sympathetic Nervous System that controls circulation, digestion, respiration, elimination, the beating of the heart. An unhealthy spine can thus affect every part of the body.

The yogi does not accept these physical changes as inevitable. He knows how to delay them and maintain good bodily condition all through his life.

The most flexible part of the spine is the neck; next is the waist; the chest and lumbar areas move least. A healthy spine may be bent forward, backward, sideways, twisted, as in Spinal Twist, or turned diagonally, as in Pose of an Archer. It may be stretched upward, compressed, flexed, tensed and relaxed.

It should be moved in all these ways every day if it is to stay in good condition. When bodily movement is limited, blood circulation is reduced. If the spine is not exercised it receives less blood, hence less nourishment; poisons and wastes are not carried away; nerves and muscles are affected. Weakness, tiredness, ill-health result. Backache is a common manifestation of this ill-health. To keep the spine healthy it must be supple; to be supple it needs correct exercise, self-manipulation and self-massage.

In yoga, physical movements are combined with the application of mental effort; with full concentration and a determination to succeed. The yogi also practises a technique known as Inversion of the Mind's Eye (see page 25). In this he learns how to 'see' his spine with the Eye of the Mind, or Third Eye, a faculty rarely developed in ordinary life.

To most people it is limited to the idle, even involuntary recreation of past scenes or absent friends, but the advanced yogi trains himself to develop it to the stage where he may use it like an X-ray, to see into his own body.

Though recognised as one of the most vital areas, in yoga the spine is not treated as a separate entity. Its relation to the other parts of the body is always taken into account, as for instance the connection between spine and sagging stomach muscles; between spine and nervous system; between spine and eliminative processes. Pressure from nervous tension, from overloaded digestive organs must be eliminated; the muscles of the trunk must be kept toned up by exercise so that they will support the spine, like a natural corset.

In the following chapters we have given some of the numerous exercises and *asanas* for conditioning the spine, but it is important to remember the inter-relationship between backbone and general system. Releasing of nervous tension and improvement of elimination are vital steps in the treatment of many back ailments.

Inversion of Mind's Eye

This mental technique, which is mentioned all through this book, should be understood before the student begins physical practice.

As in all mental exercises, steadiness of pose and breath must first be established. Sit down in a quiet place with the legs crossed, hands resting on the knees, back and neck in one straight line. Alternatively you could lie on your back. Shut the eyes and slow down the breath to the rate of about six heart beats each inhalation, six heart beats each exhalation. After a few minutes of this quiet rhythmical breathing the mind will begin to quieten, thoughts become less disorganised and receptivity increased. You will find it easier if you concentrate the mind on the point between the eyebrows – the seat of the Third Eye.

In the early stages of this technique – known as Development of the Mind's Eye – you train yourself to recreate some familiar object, in colour and full detail . . . actually to evoke this image behind your closed eyes and hold it. Start with simple things or places . . . a tree, a house, a face . . . and go on to more complex subjects.

When you feel you are mastering the exercise, turn your mind in on yourself. You must learn to 'see' inside your body, to 'see' the pockets of tension, the joints, organs, blood circulation. This is neither so unorthodox nor so impossible as it may sound. It will help if you have a knowledge of anatomy, otherwise you could study charts and photographs of the human body, familiarizing yourself with the internal structure.

The true yogi gains this knowledge by esoteric means; but the western student, though he could develop this instinctive knowledge in time, is best advised to begin as suggested above.

Relaxation

The term 'art of relaxation' which is often used, is an exact term, for ability to really relax is an art which must be studied and cultivated. *Lying down* is better than nothing but it is not enough. You should know how to methodically release tension in muscles, nerves and mind if you are to benefit.

Relaxing should be done on the floor. Spring mattresses do not permit full relaxation for when they give with the body's weight muscles instinctively tense. Lie down on a rug or carpet, on your back, with arms by the sides, feet together and eyes closed. Do not bend your arms or cross your ankles. Every muscle should be limp. The exercise you are learning is called *Savasana* – Pose of a Dead Man.

Begin by relaxing the muscles ... feet, ankles, calves, knees, thighs, hips, stomach, waistline, small of the back, right up through the body ... chest, shoulders, arms, hands, face ... lower jaw sagging, tongue relaxed, eyes rolled back under the lids, forehead smoothed out. It is not easy. Many people have no idea how to relax and find it hard to start. If you have this problem take a deep breath, clench the fists and tense the whole body, then exhale and let go. Do this a couple of times.

If you have learnt Inversion of the Mind's Eye you will find it a great help in mastering relaxation. Turn the Mind's Eye in upon yourself, searching out the areas where tension persists, making a concentrated effort to reduce it. This part of *savasana*, which comes after the muscles are relaxed, is known as Withdrawal of Nervous Energy and in it you are trying to release the inner tension, the nervous tension in the body. This is much more destructive than muscular tension and much harder to eliminate. You will not succeed by forcing but only by persuading yourself that you are letting go . . . inducing a lazy, indolent state of mind in which you do not care about anything, letting yourself sink down into the sensation that often precedes sleep. Your aim should be to *let go completely*.

Now begin to breathe the full yoga abdominal breath (see page 42). Slow down the rate of the breathing to about 6 pulse-beats each inhalation, 5 each exhalation. Slowing down the breath slows down the whole system, relaxes the nerves and releases tension.

Try to withdraw your mind from your normal surroundings . . . imagine yourself miles away in a peaceful and beautiful place where you have no cares or worries, in what yoga calls your own private *ashram* or retreat. Do not take your worries with you . . . escape them all for a brief respite. For the last minute or two, switch off *all* thoughts and keep the mind blank. This is extremely difficult but it is the means of absolute mental relaxation and refreshment.

If you can train yourself to practise *savasana*, even if only for a few minutes every day, you will soon find a remarkable difference in your health, your sleep, your outlook and your nerves in general. If your backache is caused by nervous tension it will gradually disappear.

Five minutes of correct relaxation is better than hours of restless sleep. But remember it is an exercise and you must practice to master it. It is, however, one of the greatest benefits yoga has brought to the harassed people of the west.

Elimination

We have spoken elsewhere of the connection between faulty elimination and backache, when overloaded digestive organs press on nerves or blood vessels and cause reflected pain in the back. There is also the other aspect, in which poisons retained in the system through constipation generally impair the health. If your back is your weak spot, this is where you will feel it first. The roots of the spinal nerves will be affected and the whole body will suffer.

To relieve this condition, correction of diet and eating habits is essential (too many western urban people eat too much for the work they do and too many eat too much starch); and yoga has a series of *asanas* designed to stimulate the digestive processes and improve elimination.

One, also included in this book for its benefits to the spine, is the Head-to-knee standing pose (page 51). Due to its massaging effect on the abdominal organs it corrects constipation. It should not be practised too often. Other *asanas* are Pose of a Bow (page 48); Cobra (page 47); Fish (page 63); Supine Pelvic (page 49); Locust (page 51); Spinal Twist (page 55); Pose of an Archer (pages 56–57) and the forward stretching cycle (pages 59–60).

The stomach contractions, *Uddiyana* and *Nauli* are essential for curing constipation. They should be done only on an empty stomach, preferably first thing in the morning. They are described on pages 64 and 65.

4

Preliminary Movements for the Spine

Many of the preliminary movements practised before the yoga *asanas* centre on the spine. They should be done with the eyes closed but the Mind's Eye concentrated on this area.

They are designed to limber up the backbone, to massage the roots of the spinal nerves and to keep each vertebra movable in its socket. Properly and successfully performed they are of great value to the spine. They should be learned and practised regularly by all backache sufferers not forbidden exercise.

In traditional practice, 32 movements are done very slowly. The first four are repeated four times (16); the last movement eight times from right to left, and eight from left to right (16).

All are practised in a standing position and in a very relaxed way.

1. Exercise both shoulders simultaneously in a circular movement. Bring them up, back, down, forward, smoothly and continuously. Practice four times.

2. Now reverse the movement, bringing the shoulders down, back, up, forward, still maintaining the smoothness and continuity. There should be no jerking, no quick movements interspersed with pauses. Practice four times.

This exercise massages the upper parts of the back

through the movements of the shoulder blades, and invigorates the roots of nerves in that area.

3. The second movement is called Wings. Starting with the

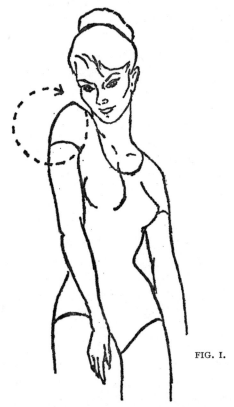

FIG. I.

fingertips on the shoulders, move the arms out from the sides in an undulating movement, bending the elbows, pushing against the air, with palms turned down.

Pressure should be felt between the shoulder blades. The

exercise stimulates the local nerve roots. Repeat four times.

4. Pagoda movement. Bring the arms up from the sides and join the palms over the head; lower the arms in front of the body, with palms still together and elbows bent. The movement should be continuous, flexible and relaxed. Repeat four times.

5. This is a most important movement. With the mind deeply concentrating on the spine, trying to 'see' it with the Mind's Eye, rotate the shoulders alternately, producing a controlled movement in every socket, working downwards, from the top to the base, then up from the base to the top. As one shoulder goes back the other begins to come forward. The exercise should be compared to swimming backstroke without arms and should be done with the same relaxed and fluid movement as those which precede it. Its object is to develop the ability *to move at will* every vertebra in its socket. Repeat four times starting with the right shoulder, then reverse and repeat four times starting with the left. (*See* Figure I).

Stretching cycle. These exercises, if practised carefully, are a great help in many backache cases and have often brought immediate relief.

Stretching up

1. Standing straight, raise the arms up over the head higher and higher, first right, then left, alternately, right, left, right, left . . . several times, as though trying to reach the ceiling, until you can stretch no more. Then completely relax, letting the arms swing limply and loosely in front of the body.

2. Stretch up in the same way but with both arms at the

same time, making the same effort to fully extend the spine; then relaxing completely.

3. Standing straight, with the arms relaxed at the sides, stretch the body itself, upwards, as though to make yourself taller. You are actually increasing your height, temporarily, as you are pulling the vertebrae apart, slightly increasing the space between them. This gives immediate relief in cases of 'pinched' spinal nerves. Inch yourself up, a fraction at a time, not just raising the head but the whole trunk, letting it become straighter and taller with each movement.

4. Stretch the spine upwards, as in number 3, above, but when fully extended start to come down, reducing your height by compressing. Once more, the spinal nerves benefit by the alternating pressure.

5. *Sideways stretching.* With arms stretched and hands clasped over the head, stretch arms and body to the right, then to the left, making the same concentrated effort to benefit the spine in the movements. We cannot over emphasise the importance of *full mental concentration* and a *full understanding of what you are doing and why.* To practice with the mind wandering about or worrying about other matters is to half-practice. Apart from yoga's teaching on the constructive power of concentration, this is only common sense, for lack of attention always results in carelessness and decreased efficiency, whatever you are doing.

It is said that apart from keeping the spine healthy, these stretching and compressing exercises could increase height, no matter what the age, if they are done daily, at the same time in the morning, without missing once, for not less than 99 days. The constructive power of the mind ... thinking tall ... is an important part of the exercise.

Rocking

A form of self-applied spinal massage, very easy to learn. (It is also recommended for overcoming insomnia, due to its soothing effect on the roots of the spinal nerves).

FIG. II.

1. Sit on a carpet, rubber mat, folded rug or blanket to protect the vertebrae from the hard floor – with the hands at the sides and legs stretched out in front. Keeping the legs together, start to rock the body back, trying to bring the legs right over the head till the toes touch the floor, then coming up and forward again into the starting position. Rock back again, and again forward ... with the movement of a rocking-chair, without jerking and keeping a smooth continuous movement.

2. Draw the knees up (with feet still on floor); put the hands under the thighs and continue the rocking.

3. Cross the legs at the ankles and take hold of the toes. Rock in this position. When you come forward continue the movement till the head touches the floor – if possible – between the feet. (*See* Figures II, IIA).

While practising the exercise keep the mind focussed on

FIG. IIA.

the spine and make sure that it receives the gentle, firm pressure of the rocking, not letting yourself roll to one side.

Spinal massage

1. Lie on the back, draw the knees up to the stomach and join your arms round them. The ankles should be crossed. Shut your eyes and in a very relaxed way rock the body from side to side ... this time the movement is like a

cradle . . . gently massaging the spine.

This simple, pleasant and beneficial exercise is always practised after such spinal *asanas* as Cobra, Bow, Locust, etc., but may be done at any time.

2. Lie on your back with your hands clasped under your neck and your knees bent and drawn up. The soles are flat on the floor. Moving them as little as possible, massage the lower back by bringing both knees right over to the left side, touching the floor, then to the right. Continue the gentle swinging of hips and legs from left to right, moving only from the waistline and keeping the upper part of the body stationary.

3. In this movement the starting position is the same as in (2) but only one leg at a time is moved. Let the left leg fall to the left, limply, till it touches the floor; bring it up and then let the right fall, to the right side. The whole character of the movements must be extreme laxness, and complete letting go of tension and muscles. Continue as long as agreeable. This is also practised as an exercise for hips and lower back.

To tone-up back muscles

Stand with the hands behind the back, level with small of the back, one hand clasping the other wrist.

Slowly bring the locked hands up the back as high as you can, tensing the back muscles, then relaxing as you lower the hands. Repeat several times, tensing and relaxing.

Movement for the hips and lower back

1. Lie on the back on the floor. Starting with the right leg

36

describe a circle by drawing the knee up towards the body, then out to the right side, then back to starting point. Repeat several times, then practice with the left leg.

2. Lie on the floor on the back with legs stretched. Raise the right leg and circle it, keeping the knee straight. Repeat several times, then circle the left leg in the same way.

3. Sit up with the legs stretched and together. Keeping both legs on the floor, move the left out to the side, while the right remains straight in front; move the left leg out further – like the hand of a clock – as far as you can, then come back to starting point. The movement is not continuous. The leg is moved a little way, then after a slight pause, moved again. Repeat with the right leg.

4. Lying on the back, circle both legs together, drawing them up with knees bent, then round, out and down. At the same time let the lower part of the body move with the legs – a kind of pivoting that massages buttocks and hips.

5. On the back, raise the left leg, keeping it straight, at right-angles with the floor; then swing it over to the right as far as possible, keeping it straight. Repeat several times. Practice the same movement with the right leg.

6. Lying on the back, perform the same movement, but this time using both legs, keeping them straight and together, swinging from side to side like a pendulum. This is a very strenuous exercise.

7. Lying on the back, draw both knees up towards the stomach, stretch the legs straight up, at right-angles to the floor – let the knees bend and the calves come down in a very relaxed way; then relax even further, and bring the

feet to the floor, in such a way that the knees – still bent – fall apart limply, one to the right, one to the left. Repeat several times.

8. Sitting up with legs stretched in front. Bring the right knee up, trying to touch it against the right shoulder. The hands rest on the floor at the sides. Repeat movement several times with the right leg; then with the left.

Strengthening of the abdominal muscles

The abdominal muscles have a great influence on the general health of the body, particularly on digestion and posture. If the muscles of the trunk should act as a corset to hold the spine in place, the abdominal muscles should be a corset for abdominal organs. Weakness and flabbiness could lead to their displacement. In some cases of extremely large stomachs, the digestive organs are literally outside the frame of the skeleton. The balance of the body is thus upset and backache is inevitable. Curvature or other spinal distortions may also result. Post-natal neglect, if allied to obesity, could create the same effect.

Yoga considers all these possibilities and the training includes many exercises for developing strong abdominal muscles. Among the most important techniques are the cycle of abdominal contractions ... *Uddiyana,* flapping *Uddiyana, Nauli* and *moving Nauli* (pages 64–65); but the muscles must be toned up and strengthened before these contractions can be practised with any success.

If any of the movements given here cause pain in the back they must be discontinued and others tried, until the right ones are found.

Where there is extreme excess weight it must be reduced.

This is imperative in every case of backache.

The exercises have been grouped as light, medium and more strenuous.

Light exercises

1. Lie down flat on the back. Alternately raise the right, then left leg to an angle of 45 degrees with the floor.
2. Lie flat on the back with the arms raised above the head. Stretch the arms and body smoothly, feeling the pulling movement in the abdomen.
3. On the back, press the right knee to the stomach with both hands, then slowly lower the leg. Press left knee to stomach and lower.
4. Press both knees together to stomach and then slowly lower. If this movement is combined with inhalation and retention of breath it brings blood to the head, producing a powerful 'flushing' effect on the brain. It is forbidden in cases of high blood-pressure.

Medium exercises

1. Lying flat on the back, with arms by the sides. Raise both legs up to an angle of 45 degrees with floor. Lower them slowly, feeling the pull on the stomach muscles.
2. Lying on the back, describe small circles with the legs, keeping them straight. Raise the legs separately as you describe the outward and upward curve of the circles, then bring them together as they come down.
3. Lying flat on the back, bring both knees up to the stomach, then stretch them up at 45 degree angle to floor and slowly lower.
4. Lying flat on the back with arms stretched above the

head. Swing the arms down and forward till palms rest on the floor at the sides, sitting up at the same time. Repeat several times, making it a continuous movement.

More strenuous

1. Lying flat on the back, clasp the hands under the neck and slowly sit up, keeping the heels on the floor.

2. Flat on the back, with the hands under the neck or at the sides. Bring the knees up to the stomach, then stretch the legs out and up to 45 degree angle, at the same time coming up into a half-sitting position. The whole movement is done quickly.

3. Lying flat on the back with arms stretched above the head. Swing the arms forward and down till the palms rest on the floor and sit up, raising the right leg to 45 degree angle at the same time. Lie back, repeat with left leg.

4. Practice the same movement, bringing both legs up at the same time.

5

Abdominal Breathing

'One who breathes correctly stays young longer.' 'To control the breath is to control life.' 'To breathe correctly is to live correctly . . .' Many more ancient yoga sayings could be quoted, all pointing to the great importance of correct breathing.

We know that breathing is the most important act of the living body. When we inhale we are oxygenating the blood stream, purifying it and providing better nourishment for the vital organs, nervous centres, glands and tissues. Abdominal breathing, the improved, complete breath of yoga which is practised with all the *asanas* or bodily poses, intensifies these benefits and at the same time enables us to increase the amount of energy or life force in the body.

When we consider the millions of breaths taken during a lifetime it is obvious that even a slight improvement in each one eventually results in better health.

Prana, cosmic energy, life force, vitality, is in the air, and according to yoga teaching is absorbed and stored in the body, increasing the vitality, endurance, energy and resistance to disease. The whole physical well-being is improved and consequently many ailments are either cured or alleviated.

There is an ancient Chinese breathing gymnastic, in

parts very similar to yoga, which teaches that breathing is the cure for all ills.

It is essential to learn the full abdominal breath of a yogi. The secret of the method is in the movements of the diaphragm, which is flattened and raised at will, enabling the lower parts of the lungs to be filled and emptied. Outwardly, this diaphragmatic movement is shown in the protrusion and withdrawal of the abdomen. The rate of breathing is very slow and all inhaling and exhaling is done through the nose, unless otherwise stated.

There are many exercises for learning the method. The following are suggested for beginners:

1. Sit with the legs crossed and palms resting on the floating ribs.

Slowly and deeply inhale and exhale, registering with your hands the expanding and contracting movements of the floating ribs and protrusion of the abdomen.

2. Practice this same deep breathing with the arms stretched above the head, palms parallel and facing each other.

3. Practice with the hands clasped behind the neck.

4. Practice with the fists clenched and pressed together behind the back.

5. Perhaps the easiest way to learn is to lie down flat on the back with the legs crossed – knees wide apart – and arms crossed behind the head ... right palm under left shoulder-blade, left palm under right shoulder-blade. Deeply inhale and exhale. It is very hard not to breathe correctly in this pose, which, due to the slight elevation it gives to the small of the back is also suggested to relieve some types of backache.

Breaths for healing and invigorating

In general yoga practice the student learns cycles of so-called Pacifying Breaths and Recharging Breaths. There are also breathing exercises dedicated to special purposes. The four given here relate, directly or indirectly, to the spine and back.

*Breathing away pain**

This is one of the yoga healing breaths.

Take half a tumbler of cold water, lie down on your back on the floor, establish slow breathing and concentrate the mind on the thought of breathing away your backache. Inhale, and as you exhale, direct *prana* to the seat of the pain, with healing effects.

This exercise, which could be used for headache, toothache, etc., is also practised sitting in cross-legged pose.

Sending prana *to the spine**

Lie down on your back on the floor with your eyes shut. Establish slow deep breathing and try to relax completely; then begin to direct *prana* to the spine and roots of the spinal nerves. Inhale, and with each exhalation send a stream of *prana* or life force to this area. At the end of the exercise the roots of the spinal nerves are warmed and refreshed.

---

* *Breathing away pain* and *Sending prana to the spine*. Despite an apparent similarity there is a subtle difference in these techniques. In the first, *prana* is used to drive out pain; in the second, *prana* is being accumulated for healing purposes. The first exercise is suitable for a transitory ailment; the second for longer-lasting conditions.

Goodwill Breath of a Yogi

This exercise, and the following one, indirectly affect the spine through improving the general condition of the body.

Yoga teaches that every cell in the body has an instinctive mind which could be brought under the command of the master mind or brain, and that complete control could be achieved through training.

Having established your position – crosslegged or lying on the back – with eyes closed and steady breathing, try to see your body as millions of cells. Then try to imagine yourself in direct contact with the instinctive minds of these cells, sending a stream of *prana* – a goodwill message – to each one with exhalation.

It is this exercise which, mastered by an advanced yogi, results in astonishing powers of self-healing.

Conversation with the Vital Organs

In yoga it is taught that, like the body cells, the vital organs may be trained to obey the Master Mind. The power is developed through persistent concentration and breath control.

Having established your pose and steady breath, concentrate on each vital organ in turn ... heart, stomach, liver, kidneys ... and with each exhalation send to them *prana* and a message of goodwill and encouragement.

6

Asanas Directly Benefitting the Spine

Yoga exercises and *asanas* are never violent; they are practised slowly, and traditionally many of the poses are held for considerable periods. No movements are undertaken until body and mind have been completely relaxed.

Strenuous exercises are always preceded by preliminary warming-up of the muscles.

A few seconds of relaxation should be allowed between each *asana*.

All *asanas* are accompanied by full yoga breathing.

Never practice for at least three hours after a heavy meal. Do not practice when overtired. Do not practice to a state of exhaustion.

All these *asanas*, which in yoga may also be practised for other purposes, should be done with the mind fully concentrated on the spine. In other words, be *aware* of the spine and what the movements and positions are doing for it, trying to get the maximum benefit from your practice.
Advasana. This is an exercise in relaxation in which the student lies flat on the floor, face downward, head turned to one side, arms limply lying by the sides. It is excellent for back conditions, especially disc troubles.
Pose of a plough. Lie on the floor, on your back, with legs together and arms by the sides. Bring the legs up, over the head and down until the toes touch the floor (*See* Figure III).

Keep the knees straight. The arms remain by the sides. Hold the pose, inhaling and exhaling, concentrating on the thought of fresh arterial blood going to the roots of the spinal nerves, of the spine itself being kept supple by this position.

To come down, slightly bend the knees, and keeping the legs together, slowly lower them until they reach the floor. Try to come down without jerking. Keep the head on the floor so that all stress is taken by back and stomach muscles. (This pose is always combined with the Candle position.)

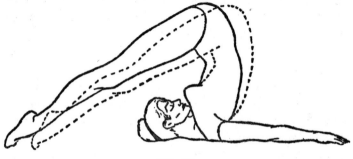

FIG. III.

Variations of the Plough pose

1. Lying on the floor, bring the legs up over the head and down towards the floor as above; but now bend the knees, take hold of the toes and stretch the legs out straight, gradually pulling them down till they touch the floor. Retain the hold on the toes, with arms and legs fully extended, while you inhale and exhale.

To come down, release the toes, lower the bent legs till they are at about right-angles with the floor; then straighten them out and come down.

46

2. Lying on the floor, link the arms loosely round the head while the legs are brought up and over into the Plough.

3. With arms linked round the head as above, bring the legs right over until toes rest on the floor. This time keep them flat, not dug into the floor. Now slide them to and fro, coming as far away and as close to the head as you can, stretching the spine. To finish, bend the knees, lower the legs to 45 degrees, straighten them out and come down to the floor. (*See* Figure III).

Choking pose. Choking pose is combined with the inverted poses, Pose of Tranquillity (page 63) and Balancing Candle (not included here), but is also practised as a separate *asana.*

Lie on the floor and bring the legs up as in *Pose of a Plough;* but as you begin to lower them over the head, separate them, bend the knees and press them to the floor, one each side of the head. The pressing is done with the hands. The feet lie flat on the floor, not with toes dug in. Hold the position for a couple of seconds, then release the pressure and lower the legs.

This pose cultivates extreme elasticity of the spine and also, through the position of the chin, puts pressure on the thyroid gland, stimulating and toning it up.

Cobra. Lie face downwards on the floor. Put the palms on the floor, level with the shoulders, and chin and feet on the floor. Inhale and raise the upper half of the trunk, *from the waistline*, with the head back. From the waist down the body must be pressed to the floor, to get the correct pressure in the small of the back. Exhale and come down. Repeat.

Then repeat twice more, with the chin pressed in as you come up.

Pose of a Bow. Lie face downwards. Bend back and take hold of your ankles. Inhale, and carefully pull on the ankles, trying to raise the legs from the floor and at the same time lifting the shoulders and upper part of the trunk. Do not jerk or pull violently. Be careful, but try to come up a little further each time. Exhale and completely relax. Practice only twice. It is very strenuous.

Pose of a Swallow. Lie face downwards on the floor with hands, one upon the other, flat under the chin. (Palms

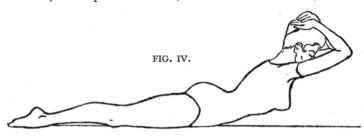

FIG. IV.

downward). Inhale and raise the body, from the waistline, at the same time stretching the arms upwards and outwards, in the movement of a swallow-dive. The feet must be kept on the floor. Exhale, return hands under the chin and relax. Repeat once or twice.

Pose of a Dolphin. Lying on the floor as in Pose of a Swallow, bring the arms forward and over the face, as shown in the illustration. One bent elbow will be fitted into the other, with the hands, one upon the other, resting on top of the head. Inhale and try to raise upper trunk, head and arms from the floor. Exhale and come down. Keep the feet on the floor. Repeat twice. (*See* Figure IV).

Modified Pose of a Fish. (For traditional full pose see Chapter 7.)

Sit with legs crossed. Arch the spine and lean back, supporting yourself with elbows, until the shoulders and back of the head are on the floor. Cross the arms behind the neck, right palm under left shoulder blade, left palm under right shoulder blade. Keep the back arched. Hold position, inhaling and exhaling.

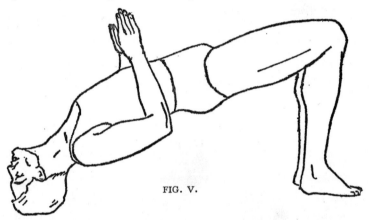

FIG. V.

Half Bridge Pose. This should be practised very carefully. Lie on the floor on your back. With a palm flat on the floor each side of the head and soles of the feet flat on the floor, try to raise up the body, arching the back, until the crown of the head rests on the floor. (*See* Figure V).

Supine Pelvic. Sit back on the heels with the hands on the knees. Lean back, supporting yourself on the elbows and coming down slowly until the crown of the head is on the floor. The spine is arched, knees kept together and on the floor, and hands held in position of prayer just below the chest.

Alternatively, split the heels and sit between them, keeping the knees together. Then arch the back and lower the head till the crown is resting on the floor.

Variations of this pose are to fold the hands under the back of the neck; to stretch the arms along the floor above the head; to fold them under the small of the back, while position is held.

Half Supine Pelvic. Sit with one leg stretched forward and the other bent back beside you. Arch the back and let yourself back and down till the head rests on the floor. Hands are in position of prayer. Repeat on other side.

While holding the pose inhale and exhale, concentrating on spinal benefits.

Pose of a Frog. Sit back on the heels with knees wide apart. The toes should be together. Raise the arms and put the palms together over the head. In this pose – a breathing position – the back is slightly arched, the head is held in line with the spine and the student concentrates on full abdominal breathing. The movement of the diaphragm and abdominal area massages and stimulates the spine.

Diamond Pose. Sit back on the heels, keeping the legs together and the palms on the knees. The head and back are in one straight line and the spine is slightly arched. Hold the pose, inhaling and exhaling, as long as comfortable.

Pose of a Child. Sitting on the heels, as above, bend forward till the forehead rests on the floor and the arms lie limply alongside the body. Hold the position, inhaling and exhaling.

Pose of a Cat. Kneel down and put your palms flat on the floor, so that arms, body and thighs form 3 sides of a rectangle. The arms should be kept straight, the head allowed to hang down. Moving only the spine, raise the back up into a hump, then let it come down, arching it; then raise again, arch again, just as a cat flexes its spine. This simple exercise is very effective if done properly. The secret is to keep the arms straight and rigid and move only the back.

PADAHASTHASANA (*Head-to-Knee Pose – Standing*). Stand with feet together and legs straight. The hands are on the backs of the thighs. Inhale, bend forward as you exhale, sliding the hands down the backs of the legs; press the face to the knees and take hold of the ankles from the back. Do not bend the knees. Repeat. The stomach should be drawn in as you come down.

PASCHIMOTTANASANA (*Head-to-Knee Pose – Sitting*). Sit with the legs stretched out in front, keeping them close together. Inhale, exhale and come forward, trying to grasp toes with the hands and pressing the face to the knees. If you cannot reach the toes, take hold of the ankles and give yourself a gentle pull down . . . be very careful if you have had slipped disc. This movement is also included as a variation of Arch Gesture (page 59).

TRIKONASANA. Stand with the legs apart and arms stretched straight out at the sides. Inhale, exhale and bend down sideways till the left hand touches the left foot. Come up and repeat on the other side.

Pose of a Locust. To be practised with care. Lying flat on your stomach, turn the head to one side. Stiffen the arms and put them under the sides, with the fists – clenched –

FIG. VI.

under the thighs. Turn the fists so that the thumbs rest on the floor. Inhale and with a quick movement raise both legs, as high as you can. Exhale and come down. The legs should be straight, the face kept on the floor. Practice twice.

Half-Locust. In this modification of the locust pose the arms are kept by the sides. With inhalation the right leg is raised, and lowered with exhalation; then the left is raised and lowered in the same way.

Pose of a Tree. (*See also Chapter* 7). Stand on the left foot. Bend the right leg back and hold the ankle in the right hand. Raise the left arm. Arch the back and look up, holding the pose as long as you comfortably can. Then come down and repeat on the other side. (This is a variation of the Tree Pose). (*See* Figure VI).

Head of a Cow Pose. Keeping the knees together, sit back on the heels, as in Diamond Pose, or sit back on the crossed ankles. Arch the back and clasp your hands behind the back. The right arm is raised with the elbow showing above the head like a crown and the right hand reaching down the back to grasp the left hand, which is pushed up from the small of the back (*See* Figure VII). Hold the pose with back well arched, inhaling and exhaling. Then lean forward, keeping hands clasped, till forehead touches the floor.

Pose of a Camel. On your knees, lean back, arching the spine; keeping the arms straight, take hold of the heels. Let the head fall back. Hold the pose as long as comfortable, inhaling and exhaling, and putting pressure on the small of the back. (*See* Figure VIII).

Sideways Swing. Sit with both legs bent to the right. Link the arms over the head. Inhale and as you exhale swing the body several times over the bent legs, moving from the waist. Sit straight, repeat inhalation-exhalation and swinging; then change legs to the other side and practice twice.

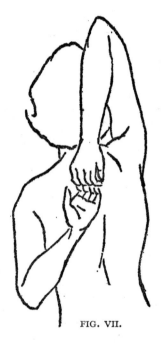

FIG. VII.

Little Twist. Sitting with the left leg stretched, step over it with the right. The right foot is flat on the floor, the right knee bent so the leg makes a triangle with the floor. The hands are at the sides. Inhale and with a quick movement swing both arms round to the right until the palms are on the floor at the right side of the body. All the movement is in the waist and small of the back. Exhale as you return. Repeat twice; then change legs and repeat twice on the other side.

Spinal Twist. Sit with the legs crossed. Press the left knee down slightly so that you can step over it with the right

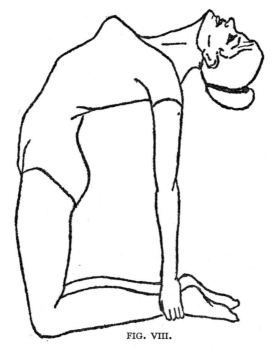

FIG. VIII.

leg. Put the right arm behind the back. Stretch the left arm in front, bring it over the right knee, still moving it to the right (and keeping it straight). Then lower it so that the hand touches the floor. Move the hand along the floor until it reaches the *right* foot. The straightened arm should be on the *right* side of the bent knee all the time. Though this may sound confusing, if

FIG. IX.

you follow carefully, step by step you will find yourself in the correct position for Spinal Twist. (*See* Figure IX).

Now inhale, exhale and twist the body right round,

slowly, from the waistline, until you can see behind you. A definite pressure should be felt in the spine and small of the back. Come forward, change sides and repeat.

Pose of an Archer. Sit in exactly the same position as for Little Twist. Inhale, exhale and lean forward, putting the left hand on the toes of the right foot (this is the leg

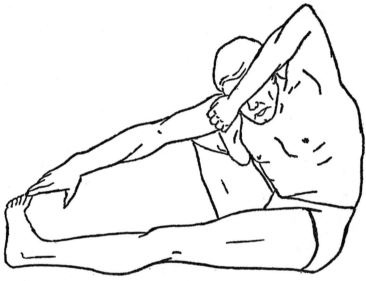

FIG. X.

stretched in front) and taking hold of the left foot with the right hand. Try to bring the left foot up till the big toe touches the forehead between the eyebrows. The right elbow (the arm that is doing the lifting) should be kept *out*, not held in close to the side. Apart from being incorrect and ugly, holding the elbow in makes the movement far more difficult. (*See* Figure X).

57

Lower the leg, change sides and repeat.

Remember the name of the *asana* . . . *Pose of an Archer*. Your movement should resemble the movement of an archer shooting an arrow from a bow.

NOTE. All the following forward-stretching *asanas* to be

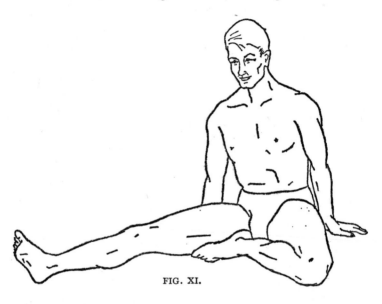

FIG. XI.

done gently and carefully without jerking, if there is any history of disc trouble.

Star Pose. Sit with the soles of the feet together and the knees wide apart. The hands rest on the ankles. Inhale, exhale and bend forward, taking hold of the feet and trying to press the forehead to the big toes. This requires extreme suppleness in the spine – which may be acquired by practice – but since it involves the muscles of the inner thigh, which are rarely used and therefore may feel the strain, it is not advisable to overdo the practice or to try forcing the body in any way.

Forward stretching cycle
Arch gesture. Sit with the left leg stretched in front and right foot pressed flat against the left thigh – knee bent and at right-angles to the stretched leg. The hands are resting on the knees.

Inhale, and as you exhale come forward till you can take hold of your left foot – or ankle – and press your head to your left knee.

Come up, repeat; then change sides and practice twice more. (*See* Figure XI).

Variation 1. With left leg stretched and right foot *under* the thigh.

Variation 2. With left leg stretched and right foot flat on the floor, knee up and close to the body, both hands resting on left knee.

Variation 3. With left leg stretched and right foot right up in the left groin, in the half-lotus position.

Variation 4. Left leg stretched and right knee bent, close to the body, foot flat on the floor. Lean forward and put your right arm *round* the bent knee and try to take hold of the left hand behind your back. Inhale, raising your head; exhale and come down till you can press your head to the left knee – still keeping the hands locked behind the back. If your hands cannot reach, use a handkerchief or scarf as extension of arm.

Variation 5. Sit with left leg stretched and right knee bent as above, but this time put the right arm *under* and through the bent leg and try to take hold of the left hand behind the back. Inhale, raise the right calf parallel to the floor, exhale and come forward till the forehead touches the knee, still keeping the hands clasped.

Variation 6. Sit with the left leg stretched and the right bent back so it lies close to the body. Hold the right ankle with the right hand, the left hand resting on the left knee. Inhale, exhale and come forward, pressing the head to the knees and touching the left foot with the left hand.

Variation 7. Sit with the left leg stretched in front and the right bent back, with the foot along the right side. The hands are clasped on top of the head. Inhale, exhale and bending body sideways, try to bring arms down over the bent leg till the right elbow touches the floor on the right side. Come up, repeat, then change legs and practice twice on the other side.

Variation 8. Sit in the same position, with the hands on top of the head. Inhale, exhale and come forward trying to bring the face down to the knees – which should be kept together – and the elbows to the floor, one on each side of the knees.

Variation 9. Sit with left leg stretched and right leg bent back as above. The right hand is on the right ankle. Inhale, arch the spine and try to come back till the head touches the floor, helping and guiding yourself with your hands on the floor at the sides. Come up, change sides and repeat.

In all these variations the movement is practised twice on the left side, twice on the right. Inhalation is done before movement, exhalation during movement. When bending forward, pull in the stomach, to help develop strong abdominal muscles.

Headstand. Although the headstand is known as the King of all yoga positions and is a most important part of yoga training, we have not included it in this book.

In itself the *asana* can only benefit those in normal health and bodily condition – it is, for instance, forbidden in cases of high blood pressure or extreme obesity – but where back troubles exist it is wiser to refrain from practice. Though in many such instances it could be harmless and beneficial, every case is different and what is safe for one may be unsafe for another.

7

Asanas Indirectly Benefitting the Spine

Although the *asanas* in this chapter do not work directly on the spine they are included for their importance to the general health and thus their indirect influence in cases of backache.

Their main benefits in this connection are mentioned throughout the book where they arise.

Aswini-mudra. Sit with the legs crossed, or sit back on the heels. Inhale, and as you exhale, contract the muscles of the anus, drawing them in. Hold contraction for a few seconds; relax; inhale, exhale again and repeat cycle. As you become used to the movement the contractions may be done more rapidly. This exercise indirectly benefits the back through helping correct haemorrhoids, prolapse, menstrual and prostate troubles, and directly through stimulating circulation in extreme lower part of spine.

Lotus position (*Buddha pose*). Restricted to those who have developed supple hip joints. Not to be forced or strained.

Sit on the floor with the legs straight. Bring left foot up till it lies in the *right* groin; then bend the right knee and bring the right foot up into the *left* groin.

The hands may be rested on the knees, or held in the lap, one upon the other, palms upward.

Shoulderstand or Candle pose. For stimulating the thyroid gland and thus invigorating whole endocrinal system. Controls weight, increases vitality, delays ageing.

Lying on the back, bring the legs up, as in pose of a Plough (page 45) but do not continue the movement down over the head. When the legs are raised as high as possible (eventually back and legs should be in one line) support the back with the hands and hold the pose, *pressing the chin to the chest* and inhaling and exhaling. If the chin is not pressed in, the arterial blood drained from legs and body will not be held at the thyroid and benefits will be lost.

To complete the *asana* bring the legs down over the head into the Plough Pose; then come down and relax.

Triangular Pose or Pose of Tranquillity. For soothing nervous system and promoting healthy sleep.

Lying on the back, stretch the arms over the head. Bring the legs up and slightly over the head, then raise the arms, keeping them straight and rest the legs on the palms. Body, arms and legs form a triangle. The weight is taken on the top of the shoulder-blades and back of the head. The pose is held by balancing. To finish the position bring the legs into the Choking Pose (page 47); come down and relax.

This *asana* usually requires practice to find the correct balance; when this is gained, hold the position as long as comfortable, deeply inhaling and exhaling.

Pose of a Fish. To relieve constipation, facilitate abdominal breathing and develop a supple spine.

Lock the legs in the Lotus position. Lean back, arching the spine, till the crown of the head rests on the floor. The

63

elbows should also touch the floor at the sides and the hands be placed on the toes.

A further modification of Fish pose is to practice, either in Lotus position, or simple crosslegged pose, with finger-tips on the solar plexus. In this position deep breathing is performed with the object of recharging the solar plexus with energy. (It is taught that some vitality or *prana* escapes from the body through the fingertips; and that the solar plexus is the storage place of energy in the body).

Balancing Poses. To improve posture.

1. Stand on the right foot with hands on hips. Place the left foot with the heel resting against the right inner ankle bone. Hold the pose with weight on one foot.

2. Bring the left foot up until the sole rests flat against the inside of the right thigh, just above the knee. Rest the left hand on the bent knee, keeping the other on the hip.

3. *Pose of a Tree.* (*See also* page 53). Try to bring the left foot up into the right groin, in half-lotus position, and retaining there raise the arms and put the palms together over the head.

When you have practised standing on the right leg, repeat movements standing on left leg. Try to hold the pose as long as you can. Try also to hold it with the eyes shut.

Stomach contractions. Essential in relieving constipation. Also alleviate menstrual difficulties and tone up all abdominal organs through deep internal massage.

To be practised only on an empty stomach. Not advisable during menstrual period, pregnancy or in cases of prolapse of uterus.

Uddiyana. Stand with feet about 18 inches apart, knees slightly bent, palms of hands resting on the thighs, with fingers facing inwards.

Inhale, completely exhale and try to draw your stomach right in and back, as though to touch the spine. At the same time press the chin to the chest and lean forward, letting your hands take some of your weight. There should be a deep hollow under the ribs.

Hold the contraction; then relax. Inhale, exhale and repeat.

When you have mastered this stage try to contract and relax the muscles alternately, making a flapping movement with the abdomen and feeling the internal massage.

May also be practised sitting cross-legged with palms on the knees.

Nauli. (Separation of abdominal recti muscles). In the same position as *Uddiyana,* after inhaling and exhaling, contract and draw in the stomach; then make a downward thrusting movement of contraction in the pit of the stomach. This – when mastered – separates the abdominal recti muscles which are rooted just above the pubic bone, and forms them into a hard column up the centre of the abdomen.

Practice until you have achieved this separation, then try to contract the muscles on the right side, forming a hard column, and on the left side. Eventually the 3 groups are contracted and relaxed one after the other, giving the external appearance of a continuous rotary movement and the internal sensation of a stimulating churning massage.

Nauli is also practised sitting in the cross-legged pose.

Continued practice – before a looking-glass – is the only way to master these important techniques.

Relaxing-breathing positions

There are 2 relaxing-breathing positions that also benefit the spine.

Lie on the right side on the floor with the right arm stretched and head resting on it, and the right knee drawn up under you. The left arm lies loosely behind the back.

Completely relax while practising full abdominal breathing.

The position is then repeated on the left side.

These poses, with *savasana* (on the back) and *advasana* (on the stomach) are yoga sleeping positions, practised with the object of improving the quality of the sleep.

Make an effort to practice *asanas*, exercises, breathing cycles or mental techniques at the same time every day, in the same place. This is the traditional procedure and helps mind and body to derive full benefits.

8

Commonsense and the Back

There is not much point trying to improve your back by special exercises if you do not give it proper care in every-day life. Too many people still regard their bodies as indestructible and are dismayed and affronted when the delicate machine breaks down. There is no need to become over-anxious or make yourself an invalid; it is mainly a matter of commonsense.

Lifting

Be careful in lifting. It is not necessarily the weight of the object that does the damage but the way it is lifted. A sudden jerk could be more harmful than a heavy weight carefully raised. Use the legs in lifting; let them take some of the stress which would otherwise be placed on the back. When stooping to lift from the floor, bend the knees. This reduces strain on the back.

Never hold or carry weights in strained or unnatural postures.

Feet

If you have corns or bunions, get them removed. If you suspect fallen arches, exercise to correct them.

Shoes

High heels are unsuitable, and uncomfortable, for standing all day behind a counter or walking for hours on hard city pavements, specially in hot weather. Women could help themselves a great deal by wearing them only at times when there will not be prolonged demands on the feet.

Go barefoot whenever possible, at home, on holidays. Walk barefoot on the carpet, on the grass, in the water. (Walking barefoot on the wet sand is an old Chinese remedy for nervous disorders). Never buy shoes that do not fit properly. There should be no pinching or cramping and there must be enough length for the toes, specially when the heels are high.

Bedding

Yoga students know that five minutes flat on the back on the floor is more refreshing than five hours in an uncomfortable bed. Sagging or lumpy beds prevent complete relaxation, for the muscles must work all the time to keep the body in position, to compensate for the displacement caused by the bed. The victim suffers from sleeplessness and backache; he has permanent muscle fatigue and having no chance to recover from the strain of his day's work gets up as tired as when he went to bed.

Oversprung are almost as bad as uncomfortable beds. The most restful form of bedding is a reasonably well-sprung mattress on a wooden platform. High pillows can distort the spine and cause pain in the back through pressure on nerves and strain on muscles and ligaments.

Sitting

Always sit well back on a chair with the weight evenly distributed and the spine straight. Do not loll or lounge about or sit in strained positions. If your work is sedentary, try to get up and move about from time to time. Alter your position as much as possible during the day. If your back is really weak you should have a chair with a proper back support until your muscles are strong enough to keep you upright without strain or fatigue.

Standing

When work entails constant standing, strain on the spine could be reduced by keeping the feet close together. This makes a better platform and improves the posture. Shift the weight from one foot to the other at times, but do not stand too long with the weight on one side. Keep the stomach well in and neck and back in one straight line. The old deportment lessons in which girls carried books on their heads were very good for the spine as well as for developing graceful carriage.

Driving

When driving long distances, stop occasionally and get out to refresh the back by walking about. Until it strengthens, support it with a cushion, but try to reach the stage where this may be dispensed with.

Chills

Never sit about in draughts when the muscles are tired. After hard physical work or exercise take a warm shower and try to rest.

Posture

In reading, do not droop over the book; hold it up towards eye level. Watch any tendency to round shoulders and check it by exercise. Watch also a disposition to let head or stomach protrude.

Other bad habits are carrying heavy bags on one side only – usually the same side (this should definitely be forbidden to growing children who often carry heavy school bags); and a practice common among young mothers – of holding the baby on one hip with the stomach pushed out to support it. It is true that this enables you to stir the custard or hold the telephone receiver with the other hand but it ruins your posture.

If you keep in mind the picture of your spine with the weight of the head balanced on it, it is easier to understand why bad posture brings pains and aches, and to resolve not to slip into it.

Rest and relaxation

Ideally, we should all have some relaxation during the day, and if one lives in a country with a siesta hour this will be feasible. For the rest of us, there is no need to abandon the thought, even if one cannot lie down on the floor in *savasana*. It is possible to learn to relax muscles and mind by slowing down the breath, while sitting in a chair, even in a bus or train. It is, of course, always best to practice *savasana* in the traditional way during the day or just before bed.

Massage

Manual spinal massage is extremely beneficial, if you

can find a masseur; but second best are the movements that massage the spine ... rocking back and forth and from side to side as described on pages 34–36.

Breathing

Yoga breathing not only keeps the body relaxed and charged with energy, it develops and benefits the abdominal and intercostal muscles, all of which affect the back. The movements of the diaphragm in inhalation-exhalation gently massage the internal organs, stimulates circulation and thus benefits general health.

Whenever possible practice breathing cycles by an open window, first thing in the morning and before bed at night.

Disc trouble

Apart from the warnings given for practising yoga in general, be careful in ordinary activities not to jerk or put sudden stresses on your spine, specially when leaning forward. Also avoid forcing or straining in any forward movements. (As an example of possible dangers to weak discs, one pupil slipped a disc by pulling her head in suddenly after leaning out a window).

Get into the habit of arching your spine while standing, encouraging the small of the back to curve inward, then flexing it outward.

Weight

Watch your weight. Do not let it contribute to backache by putting a strain on the spine. Reduce, if necessary, and train the stomach muscles to give firm support to the abdominal organs.

Diet

Increased weight, constipation, sluggishness, billious-
ness all suggest wrong diet. There are dozens of diets available, hundreds of books and articles on the subject. The
best way to reduce weight and improve health is to use
commonsense, avoid freak diets and keep to a few basic
principles.

These main principles are to replace white bread and
cakes with wholemeal bread and fruit; to eat plenty of
fresh salads and vegetables, cooked and uncooked; to
drink plenty of water and fruit juices. If there is a tendency
towards rheumatic conditions the diet should not be too
acid. Drink milk, or if you cannot, take yoghurt, butter-
milk or sour cream. If you cannot give up red meat, eat it
only once a day – less than that in hot weather. Try as
much as possible to replace it with fish, eggs, cheese.
Avoid heavy meals late at night. They cause indigestion,
insomnia and, indirectly, aching back muscles.

Elimination

Water-fasting or fruit-juice fasts are traditional methods
of purifying and resting the digestive system. Busy western
city-dwellers should limit this to one – or at most two –
days; a weekend if possible. Or substitute several days of
fruit fasting, eating only fruit.

Such fasts should only be observed once a month, and
not at all when the student is much underweight. During
the fasting, try to keep silent as much as possible, avoiding even the telephone; take it easy in general and go to
bed early. An enema at the end of the day is part of the
traditional observance.

Periodical fasts, with regular daily practice of stomach contractions and correction of diet will cure constipation.

Sunbaths

Sunbathing relaxes the spinal nerves and allows the sun's vitamin D to reach the skin. It is highly beneficial but not when carried to the point of exhaustion or severe sunburn.

Sex

Over-indulgence in sex can bring on chronic backache, and constant stimulation without satisfaction may result in pains in the lumbar region. When back trouble already exists certain coital postures should be avoided . . . the so-called normal position puts considerable strain on the man's back and could be damaging. In such cases individual adjustments should be made.

Mental attitude

In overcoming illness and painful conditions, perseverence and confidence in yoga's power to heal are essential. A positive attitude to any problem, backache included, is a powerful weapon for final victory.

As for those pains that have their origins in mental or emotional disturbances, though we cannot always solve the problems that cause them, we can, if we wish, allow yoga to help. When the body is healthy, the nerves relaxed, the glands and circulation working properly and the system free of impurities there is a remarkable feeling of well-being, irrespective of circumstances. This physical well-being communicates with and influences the mind, bringing increased optimism, fortitude and in general a more relaxed attitude towards life; while those who go further upon the path of spiritual development will find serenity and peace, as well as freedom from their aches and pains.

Appendix

Spinal Massage

'Run your fingers along my spine and I will purr like a cat.'
From a Chinese poem.

In the history of civilization, spinal massage for pleasure or therapeutic purposes has always featured, particularly in the East. It is mentioned in the literature of China, Japan, Persia, India and Arabia.

The most outstanding form is the Chinese three-fold massage. The name comes from the continuous repetitions of pressures and massaging movements on the spine. The duration of the massage varies according to the nature of the ailment and must be decided by the masseur.

The process is designed to invigorate the roots of the spinal nerves and through them to tone up the entire inner life of the body. It produces an immediate sensation of physical well-being which often lasts for a considerable time.

Apart from these invigorating properties, it has been credited with many spectacular cures in cases of paralysis, impotence and ulcers. Sister Kenny's treatment of poliomyelitis was largely based on the principles used in this Chinese system.

The masseur's art is usually a family preserve, passed down from generation to generation, but occasionally an

75

outsider may learn the technique. Michael Volin was taught by a famous Chinese masseur in Shanghai.

Skilled masseurs are so greatly in demand that there is often a long waiting-list for their services. The treatment is always expensive and hard to obtain in the East, for due to the demanding nature of the work a good masseur can give only a limited number of treatments a day. At the end of each he is often exhausted, so great is the expendi-

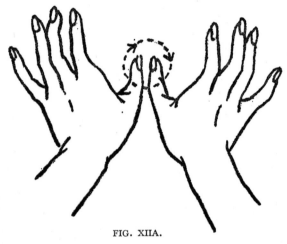

FIG. XIIA.

ture of vital energy. Provision must be made for rest and recharging, between patients.

The massage is always done in the traditional manner.

The patient lies on a low table or on the floor, face downwards, head turned to one side, hands at the sides, palms *up*. The feet are about 12 inches apart.

The masseur kneels with one knee between the patient's parted thighs, the other outside the right or left thigh.

Placing his palms on the patient's lumbar region, and using his thumbs, he massages the last joint of the lower vertebrae, three times, with a circular movement – clockwise. (*See* Figure XIIA). Then, using the same movement,

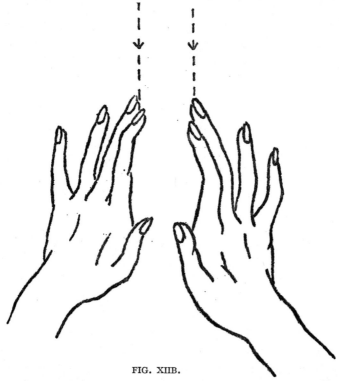

FIG. XIIB.

he works higher up the spine, applying firm but gentle pressure, massaging still in a clockwise movement till he reaches the top vertebra of the back (excluding the neck).

Continuous pressure is then applied down each side of the spine, using the second finger of each hand (the finger next to the index finger). (*See* Figure XIIB). One finger is placed on each side of the top vertebra and drawn right down to the bottom with a firm but gentle pressure. This is done three times.

Now, using the thumbs again, each vertebra is massaged three times in an up-and-down (not clockwise) movement.

The whole procedure is repeated three times ... the circular massaging movement working up the spine; the sustained pressure of the fingers coming down; the up-and-down massaging movement.

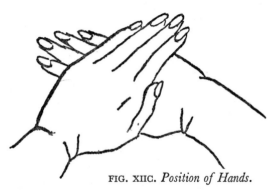

FIG. XIIC. *Position of Hands.*

With the left palm on the back of the right hand the masseur presses three times on each vertebra with the flat of the hand. (*See* Figure XIIc). He starts at the bottom and moves up the spine. The direction of the hands is changed after each pressure ... fingers overlapping the spine to the right, then overlapping to the left, and so on all the way up.

This cycle could be repeated as many times as the masseur feels necessary for the particular complaint.

Every case requires an individual approach. The strength of the pressure depends on the build, sex and age of the patient. Large, corpulent people with a heavy layer of fat over the spine need more pressure than those who are thinner.

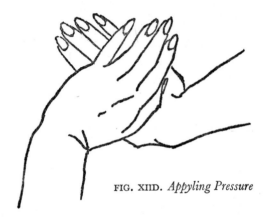

FIG. XIID. *Appyling Pressure*

This technique could be learnt by a husband and wife and applied to each other. A very important part of the treatment is the masseur's desire to relieve pain through loving care, and the patient's undoubted faith in its power to help him.